THE
COLD WAR

Essential Events

THE COLD WAR

BY KAYLA MORGAN

Content Consultant
Richard Filipink
Associate professor, History Department
Western Illinois University

ABDO
Publishing Company

CREDITS

Published by ABDO Publishing Company, 8000 West 78th Street,
Edina, Minnesota 55439. Copyright © 2011 by Abdo Consulting
Group, Inc. International copyrights reserved in all countries. No
part of this book may be reproduced in any form without written
permission from the publisher. The Essential Library™ is a
trademark and logo of ABDO Publishing Company.

Printed in the United States of America,
North Mankato, Minnesota
062010
092010

♻ THIS BOOK CONTAINS AT LEAST 10% RECYCLED MATERIALS.

Editor: Melissa Johnson
Copy Editor: Nick Cafarelli
Interior Design and Production: Emily Love
Cover Design: Christa Schneider

Library of Congress Cataloging-in-Publication Data
Morgan, Kayla.
  The cold war / Kayla Morgan.
     p. cm. — (Essential events)
  Includes bibliographical references and index.
  ISBN 978-1-61613-681-9
  1. Cold War—Juvenile literature. I. Title.
  D843.M685 2011
  909.82'5—dc22
                                        2010009926

TABLE OF CONTENTS

LAUNCH POSITION

MISSILE-READY TENTS

MISSILE ERECTORS

Spy photo showing a missile base in Cuba during the Cuban Missile Crisis

STANDOFF

or two tense weeks in October 1962, the world faced the real possibility of a nuclear war. The United States and the Soviet Union faced off in a conflict over the presence of nuclear missiles on the island nation of Cuba. Cuba is only 90 miles

(45 k) south of Florida. At the time, Cuba and the United States were not on good terms with one another.

Cuba was allied with the Soviet Union, which had begun moving missiles into Cuba in the summer of 1962. When the U.S. government realized that these missiles were active and pointed to launch toward major U.S. cities, it demanded that the Soviets remove them at once. The Soviets refused. At first they denied the missiles' existence. Then they claimed the missiles were necessary to protect the island from U.S. aggression.

The Cuban Missile Crisis became a standoff. If the Soviets fired their missiles out of Cuba toward the United States, the Americans promised to fire theirs in return. The Soviet Union would do the same if the United States attacked first. But these nuclear weapons were so powerful that if either nation fired,

The USSR

The USSR, or Soviet Union, was formed by Vladimir Lenin after the Bolshevik Revolution of 1917. The Soviet Union was a group of Communist republics that Lenin united to form a larger nation. The structure was in some ways similar to that of the United States. In the United States, each state has its own government but ultimately answers to the national leadership. The Soviet republics that made up the Soviet Union were subordinate to the central government. The republics had less independence than U.S. states do, however.

The Soviet Union included Russia, Ukraine, Belorussia, Moldavia, Azerbaijan, Armenia, Georgia, Kazakhstan, Uzbekistan, Turkmenistan, Kirgiziva, Tajikistan, Estonia, Lithuania, and Latvia.

The Soviet Union also controlled several allied nations called satellite states. These states also had little independence.

the other was likely to be completely destroyed.

During this crisis, U.S. President John F. Kennedy and Soviet Premier Nikita Khrushchev faced decisions that world leaders had not faced before and would help define each of their legacies. But the stage for this crisis was set long before either man came to power.

THE UNITED STATES VERSUS THE SOVIET UNION

The United States and the Soviet Union had a complex relationship. By the mid-twentieth century, they were the most powerful nations in the world. Each was strong politically and militarily, but their governments' approaches to running a nation were very different. Each country's leaders respected the other, but they did not always agree. Each country wanted to be seen as acting justly, and each wanted other nations around the

John F. Kennedy

John Fitzgerald Kennedy was born on May 29, 1917, in Brookline, Massachusetts, to a wealthy Irish Catholic family. He graduated from Harvard University in 1940 and joined the U.S. Navy in 1941. He served bravely in World War II and was honored for his service.

After the war, Kennedy became a Democratic representative from Massachusetts and then a senator. In 1960, he became the youngest man ever elected president of the United States. As president, Kennedy's clashes with the Soviets included conflicts over Cuba, the German city of Berlin, and Vietnam. On November 22, 1963, Kennedy was shot and killed by an assassin while riding in a motorcade in Dallas, Texas. He was 46 years old.

world to be on its side when it fought with the other.

These two powerful nations had fought as allies during World War II (1939–1945). After the war, however, their very different political ideologies set them apart. The Soviet Union, whose official name was the Union of Soviet Socialist Republics (USSR), had a Communist economy and an authoritarian system of government. Under the Soviet system of communism, individuals did not have private property. The central government owned most of the property, businesses, and industries in the nation. The government also exercised a lot of control over people's jobs, wages, and lifestyles.

The United States had a capitalist economy and republican system of government. Individual citizens owned most of the property, businesses, and industries in the nation. Instead of controlling jobs,

Nikita Khrushchev

Nikita Khrushchev was born on April 17, 1894, in a province of what is now Ukraine. He served as a political officer with the Red Army.

Khrushchev became the leader of the Soviet Union in 1955. As premier, he was known for his diplomacy. Khrushchev softened or reformed some of the harsh laws that controlled the Soviet citizens. He discussed nuclear disarmament with U.S. leaders.

Khrushchev lost power in 1964 after a coup by members of his government. He died on September 11, 1971.

wages, and businesses, the government allowed a free market to develop.

THE COLD WAR

The U.S. capitalist system and the Soviet Communist system did not coexist well. When World War II ended in 1945, many European nations suffered from war damage and needed to rebuild homes, businesses, factories, schools, and other structures. Some nations also faced economic and political challenges. Some governments had collapsed entirely. Countries that were already suffering from the Great Depression of the 1930s now faced additional economic hardships brought on by the war.

Americans wanted these countries to become capitalist, with new businesses participating in a free-market economy with U.S. businesses. The Soviets wanted these countries to become their allies, preferably under Communist systems. Both the United States and the Soviet Union tried to influence European governments to follow their ideologies. Physical and ideological battle lines were drawn in Europe and around the world. For the next 45 years, the two superpowers would fight to keep

Cuban president Fidel Castro, left, and Soviet leader Nikita Khrushchev, right, at the United Nations General Assembly in 1960

control of their territory and to gain new ground where they could.

This conflict between the United States and the Soviet Union is called the Cold War because the heart of the fighting took place in political games,

not armed warfare. This kind of
war stood in sharp contrast to the
battlefield fighting that had just taken
place in Europe and the South Pacific
during World War II. However, the
conflict was no less serious, as was
shown during those tense October
days of 1962 that became known as
the Cuban Missile Crisis.

THE CUBAN MISSILE CRISIS

The president of Cuba, Fidel
Castro, believed strongly in
communism. This was good news
for the Soviets. It gave them an ally
very close to the United States. They
would try to take advantage of this
opportunity.

In August 1962, the director of
the U.S. Central Intelligence Agency
(CIA) reported to President Kennedy
that he suspected the Soviets were
moving missiles into Cuba. The
president ordered spy planes to fly
over Cuba and take pictures of the

"Neither the United States
of America nor the world
community of nations can
tolerate deliberate decep-
tion and offensive threats
on the part of any nation,
large or small. . . . Nuclear
weapons are so destruc-
tive and ballistic missiles
are so swift, that any
substantially increased
possibility of their use or
any sudden change in
their deployment may
well be regarded as a
definite threat to peace."[1]

—*John F. Kennedy,
Cuban Missile
Crisis address,
October 22, 1962*

landscape. The mission took place on October 14, 1962. When the planes returned, they carried bad news: The Soviets had installed missiles that would be ready to launch in a matter of days.

President Kennedy wanted to threaten an attack on Cuba, or the Soviet Union itself, but he did not want to have to follow through on it. Kennedy spent a week consulting with aides, keeping his knowledge of the missiles secret from the public. Next, he sent U.S. military ships to surround Cuba, blocking any new

Cuba

The island of Cuba, located in the Caribbean, was first populated by native peoples. Christopher Columbus's ships landed at Cuba in 1492, and soon after that the island was colonized by Spain. The island remained a Spanish colony for centuries.

In 1898, the United States backed an independence movement by the Cuban people. The conflict became known as the Spanish-American War. After the war, Spain lost its control over the island. From the turn of the twentieth century until the late 1950s, Cuba was an independent nation ruled by a series of military regimes.

In 1959, Fidel Castro led a rebel army to victory. He led the country for nearly 50 years, installing a Communist government that was supported by the Soviet Union for some of that time. Under President Kennedy, the United States created a law forbidding trade with Cuba. After the end of the Cold War, Cuba began to suffer from the missing Soviet aid and the absence of U.S. trade, which created greater poverty in the country. Today, thousands of Cuban refugees try to reach the United States by boat each year.

In 2008, Fidel Castro resigned, turning the presidency over to his brother, Raúl Castro. Cuba remained a Communist nation in 2010.

Soviet shipments from arriving. This "quarantine" of Cuba, as it was called, angered Castro and the Soviets, but they did not try to pass the line of U.S. ships.

During the next week, tense negotiations took place between U.S. and Soviet officials. Each nation threatened to bomb the other. No one wanted to follow through on these threats, but the leaders did not want to be seen as weak, either. It was a terrifying time for people in both nations. Some citizens were sure that the world as they knew it was about to end.

Fortunately, neither superpower acted on its threats. The Soviets sent a back-channel communication to President Kennedy, offering a peaceful settlement. Khrushchev promised to withdraw the Soviet missiles from Cuba if Kennedy promised never to invade the Communist island. President

"We're eyeball to eyeball, and I think the other fellow just blinked."[2]

–Secretary of State Dean Rusk, learning of the Soviet offer to stand down during the Cuban Missile Crisis

Kennedy agreed to the terms, while also privately agreeing to remove U.S. missiles from Turkey. Both sides backed down while maintaining their status as superpowers. The crisis ended, and nuclear war was avoided.

ONE SMALL BATTLE, ONE BIG WAR

The Cuban Missile Crisis is a dramatic example of how the Cold War played out. The United States and the Soviet Union were engaged in a constant standoff that sometimes flared up into critical situations. People on both sides of the conflict believed nuclear war was a possibility at any time. It was a time of great fear, suspicion, and protectiveness. People's daily lives were overshadowed by a powerful, invisible threat.

The Cuban Missile Crisis was one of many incidents that very nearly turned the Cold War hot. However, one crisis held off could not undo years of deep-seated distrust between

U-2 Spy Planes

President Kennedy sent U-2 spy planes to fly over Cuba. These high-altitude surveillance jets were each fitted with a camera. The pilot would turn the camera on at the right time, and it would automatically snap photos of whatever was below. Afterward, the long strip of film would be collected and each frame reviewed by experts. These planes were used frequently throughout the Cold War to gain intelligence about Soviet military movements.

the two superpowers. The Cold War would continue
until the late 1980s, and more confrontations
between the two nations would set the world
on edge. ⌐

President John F. Kennedy addressed the nation about the Cuban Missile Crisis on October 22, 1962.

U.S. and Soviet soldiers shake hands during World War II.

THE IRON CURTAIN

During World War II, the leaders of the Soviet Union, Great Britain, and the United States formed an alliance to fight Adolf Hitler's Germany, which was trying to take over Europe. This group was known as the Allies. At the time, Germany was a powerful threat to all three nations, as well as many other countries around the world. By the summer of 1940, Germany had conquered much of Europe. The United States officially joined the war in December 1941. The United States also fought Japan in the Pacific Ocean.

Even though these three nations called themselves Allies, they did not all have the same interests or long-term goals. They did not join forces because they completely agreed with one another. They united because they all wanted to stop Germany's expansion. The United States and the Soviet Union, especially, had a shaky partnership.

Once it became clear that the Allies were going to defeat Germany and reclaim European lands, the cooperation between the Allied nations began to fall apart.

ALLIES TO ADVERSARIES

In the years immediately following World War II, the United States and the Soviet Union shifted from allies to adversaries. A deep-rooted resentment still existed between the two nations over decades-old political issues. The Soviet Union, led by Premier Joseph Stalin, was deeply committed to authoritarian

Joseph Stalin

Joseph Stalin, born in 1879, was the leader of the Soviet Union during World War II. He was a harsh dictator during his time in power (1929–1953) and executed or jailed people who spoke against him. He revolutionized industry and farming in the country by forcibly taking over private companies. He murdered anyone who opposed him. His secret police spread terror among the people and the members of the Communist Party alike.

During World War II, Stalin initially aligned the Soviet Union with Hitler's Germany, but he joined the Allies when the Germans attacked Soviet lands. After the war ended, Stalin gradually cut off communications with Western Europe and the United States. He died in 1953.

communism. The United States, led by President Harry S. Truman, was just as deeply committed to democratic capitalism. It seemed that the two systems could not be reconciled.

During the war, Britain and the United States liberated the Western European nations such as France, the Netherlands, Belgium, and Austria from the Germans. The Allies returned self-rule to the citizens of each country. The Soviet Union took control of the Eastern European nations, including Poland, Hungary, Romania, and Czechoslovakia. However, the Soviets did not let go of control of those nations. Instead, they closed the borders and turned them into Communist states.

The Allies also divided Germany. They agreed that power could not be handed back to the Germans immediately, or the war might flare

Many of the countries of Eastern Europe, shown in red circa 1946, were controlled by the Soviet Union during the Cold War.

up again. The Soviets took the eastern section of the nation, and France, Britain, and the United States shared control of the western section. The German capital, Berlin, was also divided among the Allies, though the city rested deep in the Soviet-controlled section of the country.

At first, these divisions were friendly. Within a few short years, however, Berlin would become the site of the first Cold War showdown.

Capitalism vs. Communism

The division between capitalism and communism was complex. Communists believed their way was best because it gave workers power and promoted equality, so the wealthy could not take advantage of the poor. Capitalists believed their way was best because the free market encouraged people to compete for wealth, which made them work harder and create better products.

Under the ancient, class-based feudal system in Europe, a person born into nobility would always be noble. A person born to a peasant would always be a peasant. There was no way to change social stations. Capitalism changed society. Classes still existed, but they were less formal and each person's place in them became less permanent. A poor farmer could work hard and hope to become a rich farmer; a textile-factory worker could save his money and perhaps one day open his own clothing store. A capitalist economy would grow because people put their ideas and new products into the marketplace.

According to nineteenth-century political thinker Karl Marx, capitalism was still a very class-based system. Under capitalism, Marx said, society's poorest people were not allowed to compete in the

Karl Marx's writings formed much of the basis for communism.

market in a meaningful way. Their only option was to sell their labor. The upper classes, such as business owners and factory owners, bought that labor and profited from it, while paying the workers very little in return. Marx believed this system could not last. Just as peasants grew tired of the

The Communist Manifesto

Karl Marx and Friedrich Engels wrote *The Communist Manifesto*, which was first published in 1848. It argues, "The history of all hitherto existing society is the history of class struggles. Hitherto, every form of society has been based, as we have already seen, on the antagonism of oppressing and oppressed classes."[1] The document reports on the nature of class struggles and how the oppressed classes should work to overcome them.

feudal system and revolted to create capitalism, workers would tire of capitalism, revolt, and ultimately create communism. Under Marx's ideal of communism, property would be held collectively by the people and goods would be distributed fairly. Marx's writings and theories about government and society formed much of the basis for communism as it existed during the twentieth century.

The Soviet Communist Party's belief in Marx's teachings was so strong that the party forcibly tried to bring about communist revolutions in other countries. U.S. capitalists, on the other hand, continued to disagree with Marx's vision. Instead, they encouraged those countries to join the free market.

The Iron Curtain

The capitalist and Communist nations of the world were on a collision course. As the Allied superpowers divided up European territory and partitioned Germany, the ideological split became more and more obvious.

On March 5, 1946, in Fulton, Missouri, Winston Churchill, Britain's prime minister during World War II, gave a now-famous speech. He cautioned Americans of the trouble ahead. Speaking of the condition of Europe, he said, "From Stettin in the Baltic to Trieste in the Adriatic an iron curtain has descended across the Continent."[2] Churchill's "iron curtain" description would

Churchill's Iron Curtain Speech

Churchill's 1946 speech described the line between the Soviet Union and Western Europe.

It is my duty . . . to place before you certain facts about the present position in Europe. From Stettin in the Baltic to Trieste in the Adriatic an iron curtain has descended across the Continent. Behind that line lie all the capitals of the ancient states of Central and Eastern Europe.

Warsaw, Berlin, Prague, Vienna, Budapest, Belgrade, Bucharest and Sofia; all these famous cities and the populations around them lie in what I must call the Soviet sphere, and all are subject, in one form or another, not only to Soviet influence but to a very high and in some cases increasing measure of control from Moscow.

The safety of the world, ladies and gentlemen, requires a unity in Europe, from which no nation should be permanently outcast. . . .

I repulse the idea that a new war is inevitable—still more that it is imminent. It is because I am sure that our fortunes are still in our own hands and that we hold the power to save the future, that I feel the duty to speak out now that I have the occasion and the opportunity to do so.[3]

soon come to describe the boundary between capitalism and communism in Europe. But the Cold War had already begun.

The Nuclear Threat

By the spring of 1945, the Allies had won the war in Europe, but the battle in the Pacific continued. The U.S. military felt confident of victory, but the Japanese refused to surrender. The Japanese appeared willing to fight until every last soldier had given his life for the cause. In hopes of ending the war faster and saving the lives of U.S. soldiers, Truman authorized the dropping of atomic, or nuclear, bombs on two Japanese cities, Hiroshima and Nagasaki. The bombs were dropped over civilian populations in August to scare the Japanese into an immediate surrender. The Japanese surrendered shortly after. In part, Truman's legacy as president was defined by his decision to use atomic weapons.

The use of nuclear weapons also served as a signal to the Soviet Union. The Soviets knew that if they wanted to compete with the United States for global domination, they, too, needed nuclear bombs at the ready.

*The atomic bombs caused incredible devastation
in Hiroshima and Nagasaki.*

President Truman wanted to stop the spread of communism.

THE TRUMAN DOCTRINE

The United States hoped never to use the atomic bomb again or, worse yet, to have such bombs used on its own citizens. The next several decades in U.S. political life were largely dedicated to preventing nuclear war, though sometimes U.S. leaders took action in roundabout ways.

Soviet military technology would soon match that of the United States. Perhaps the best course of action, the U.S. government reasoned, was to find as many capitalist allies as possible around the world. Under President Truman, U.S. foreign policy shifted to focus on preventing the spread of communism. This became known as containment.

CONTAINMENT

Truman believed that the United States had a moral duty to protect its allies from the spread of communism. He called this policy "containment." The goal was to keep communism contained within the Soviet Union and the places where it already existed. Rather than trying to convert Communist nations to capitalism, U.S. energy would be spent on maintaining the status quo. The iron curtain would remain fixed where it was.

"I believe that it must be the policy of the United States to support free peoples who are resisting attempted subjugation by armed minorities or by outside pressure."[1]

—*President Harry S. Truman, on establishing his Truman Doctrine*

The Soviets had a different approach. They did not wish to "contain" capitalism—their goal was to spread communism, and they had their eyes set on southern Europe and the Middle East. Soviet troops massed on Turkey's border, while Soviet-backed Communists attempted to seize power in Greece. Both Turkey and Greece were traditionally protected by Great Britain, however.

In March 1947, Truman asked Congress to provide $400 million in military aid to Greece and Turkey. Truman articulated his vision for the nation, saying that it was the American duty to stand up and defend free people around the world from the threat of Soviet communism. This vision became known as the Truman Doctrine. By and large, the nation agreed with him. The funds were approved. The noncommunist Greeks prevailed in their civil war, while the Soviets backed off from Turkey.

U.S. involvement in this instance raised serious questions for the president and Congress. Was U.S. protection against communism abroad a one-time event? Did the Truman Doctrine apply only to Greece and Turkey? To all of Eastern Europe? Or to the whole world?

THE MARSHALL PLAN

President Truman called in his advisers to help him solidify the Truman Doctrine and figure out how to enforce the containment policy. On June 5, 1947, the United States announced a plan to send economic aid to Europe for its recovery. The plan was soon dubbed the Marshall Plan, after Secretary of State George C. Marshall, a former general. Marshall was one of the plan's main creators and supporters.

The central purpose of the Marshall Plan was to help European governments

Harry S. Truman

Harry S. Truman was born in 1884 in Lamar, Missouri. He served as a field artillery captain in France during World War I. Truman later became active in the Democratic Party as a judge and then became a Missouri senator in 1934. He headed the Senate war-investigating committee during World War II and monitored military spending. He was elected vice president under President Franklin Delano Roosevelt in 1944.

Roosevelt died suddenly on April 12, 1945, and Truman assumed the presidency at a crucial time in U.S. history. With the armed forces still caught up in World War II, he faced significant challenges as commander in chief. Almost immediately upon taking office, he was confronted with the decision to drop the atomic bombs on Japan. He soon faced off with the Soviets in Berlin, sent U.S. troops around the world to protect democracy and fight communism, and established domestic aid programs under the Fair Deal. He helped establish the United Nations and NATO and presided over the conflict in Korea. Truman completed his presidency in 1953. He died on December 26, 1972.

rebuild their economies. U.S. leaders hoped their aid would help encourage these nations to maintain free-market economies. Between 1948 and 1951, the United States provided more than $12.5 billion in aid to Europe, which helped the national economies recover much faster than they would have without assistance. In 1949, the program was expanded to include aid to developing nations. Again, the goal was to prevent communism from taking root and to shape fledgling governments.

North Atlantic Treaty Organization

President Truman did not intend for Americans to fight the Soviet power single-handedly, however. He worked with other procapitalist world leaders to form the North Atlantic Treaty Organization, or NATO. Twelve nations initially joined the

Current NATO Members

As of 2010, the North Atlantic Treaty Organization had 28 members, many of whom either did not exist yet or were under Soviet influence when the first North Atlantic Treaty was signed in 1949. NATO's 28 members are: Albania, Belgium, Bulgaria, Canada, Croatia, the Czech Republic, Denmark, Estonia, France, Germany, Greece, Hungary, Iceland, Italy, Latvia, Lithuania, Luxembourg, the Netherlands, Norway, Poland, Portugal, Romania, Slovakia, Slovenia, Spain, Turkey, the United Kingdom, and the United States.

group, which became official on April 4, 1949. In addition to the United States, the member nations included the United Kingdom, Belgium, Canada, Denmark, France, Iceland, Italy, Luxembourg, the Netherlands, Norway, and Portugal. Within the next six years, Greece, Turkey, and a newly formed West Germany joined the coalition.

NATO countries agreed to respond together if any single nation among them was attacked. They would also come to each other's aid in a crisis. In 1950, President Truman sent troops to Europe to serve as NATO's armed forces. NATO's governing body, the North Atlantic Council, named General Dwight D. Eisenhower as NATO supreme commander.

The Warsaw Pact

After West Germany joined NATO in 1955, the Soviet Union joined with seven of its satellite states and formed its own procommunist version of NATO. Signed in May, the agreement became known as the Warsaw Pact, after the capital of Poland, where the treaty meeting took place. The member nations, in addition to the Soviet Union, were Albania, Bulgaria, Czechoslovakia, East Germany,

The Warsaw Pact

Although the NATO treaty still existed in 2010, the Warsaw Pact did not. After the fall of the Soviet Union, the member nations found the treaty pointless. The pact was officially dissolved in 1991 in Prague, Czech Republic, as the new democratic governments of each nation chose not to re-sign.

Hungary, Poland, and Romania. Like the NATO agreement, the Warsaw Pact nations committed to treating an attack against one as an attack against them all. With that, the battle lines of the Cold War were drawn.

Soviet leaders met to discuss and sign the Warsaw Pact.

Soviet leader Joseph Stalin wanted to retain control of East Berlin.

MILITARY MOBILIZATION

mmediately after World War II, military
tensions between the United States and
the Soviet Union were handled through diplomacy.
The two nations were still allies, at least in name,
so they treated each other politely and with respect.

U.S. intervention in Greece and Turkey had sent
a message to the Soviets. Stay behind your line,
Truman had warned, or we will fight you. Stalin
received the message loud and clear. But he was
committed to spreading communism, so he was
willing to take on that fight.

THE BERLIN BLOCKADE

The division of Germany established at the end
of World War II left eastern Germany in Soviet
control and western Germany controlled by the
United Kingdom, France, and the United States.
The western portion had been divided into three
sectors—one for each country—but now the leaders of
these countries wanted to unite the sectors to create
a single democratic state in West Germany. This plan
did not sit well with Stalin.

In 1948, Stalin ordered his forces to stop the
Western powers from accessing Berlin, the capital
of Germany. The Soviet Union held control of East
Berlin, but the United Kingdom, France, and the
United States controlled the western half of the city,
even though it was located in the part of Germany
under Soviet control. On June 24, 1948, the Soviets
blockaded West Berlin, blocking off all roads and

Cold War Battles Worldwide

The Korean and Vietnam wars, the Berlin Blockade, and the Berlin Wall are among the more famous events of the Cold War. U.S. troops were also part of a worldwide struggle. The United States stepped into conflicts in Central and South America, the Suez Canal, Afghanistan, and throughout the Middle East, in addition to other smaller fights that seemed minor compared to the large-scale military efforts in Korea and Vietnam. In some cases, the United States minimized its involvement by backing democratic efforts in secret.

waterways that led into or out of the city.

The blockade angered Truman and the other Western leaders, and it was a disaster for the citizens of West Berlin. They were trapped—no food or supplies could be brought in.

Under the Truman Doctrine, the United States could not stand by and allow the Soviets to blockade West Berlin. Truman ordered supplies to be delivered to the city by airlift. U.S. and British aircraft began dropping supplies to residents on June 26. The planes flew constantly, bringing food, medical supplies, and other essentials.

Most historians consider the Berlin Blockade the first battle of the Cold War. After nearly a year, the Soviets backed down and lifted the blockade on May 12, 1949.

The Korean War

After World War II, Korea had split into Soviet-allied North Korea and U.S.-allied South Korea.

On June 24, 1950, Communist forces from North
Korea supported by the Soviet Union and China
invaded South Korea, a procapitalist nation.
President Truman sent U.S. soldiers to support
the South Koreans. He also appealed to the United
Nations (UN) to send assistance. The UN troops,
mostly American, fought in what was officially called
a "police action." War was never declared, although
fighting was fierce.

U.S. Army General Douglas MacArthur led the
UN troops as they pushed the North Koreans back
into their own territory. MacArthur supported the
Truman Doctrine's containment policy, but he
wanted to take the conflict a step further. Pushing
the Communists back into the North was not enough
for him. He hoped to conquer the entire Korean
peninsula. With Truman's permission, MacArthur
attempted to invade North Korea in the fall of 1950.

The Soviet Union and China, also a Communist
nation, helped the North Koreans. In November,
Chinese forces entered the fighting on the side of
North Korea. The UN troops were driven back, and
the conflict turned into a stalemate. Truman began
negotiations with the Chinese in 1951, but he failed
to reach a settlement. A cease-fire agreement was

finally reached in 1953 by Dwight D. Eisenhower, who followed Truman as U.S. president. North Korea remained Communist. South Korea remained friendly to the capitalist West, but the nation had sustained heavy losses in human life and property damage.

The settlement raised controversy at home. Many Americans, including MacArthur and his supporters, believed that the United States should have pushed harder to take control of North Korea, despite the massive casualties the UN troops sustained.

The Berlin Wall

Meanwhile, the situation in East Germany was increasingly tense. The divided city of Berlin was feeling the strain of capitalism versus communism, especially because the two systems of government existed side by side. Funds from the Marshall Plan supported West Berlin, boosting

Dwight D. Eisenhower

President Eisenhower was a war hero and well-known personality long before he became president of the United States. He was a strong military leader during World War II, and when the Allied troops invaded France, Eisenhower was their supreme commander. Later, he became the first supreme commander of NATO. Eisenhower went by the nickname Ike, and his presidential campaign slogan in 1952 was, "I like Ike."[1]

*Workers add glass shards to the top of the Berlin Wall
to stop East Berliners from escaping.*

its economy and making it a desirable place to live.
Soviet control in East Berlin remained harsh and
repressive.

In the early 1950s, travel between the two sides of
the city was open. People from East Germany began
to flow into West Berlin, where they could easily
then travel to West Germany and beyond. Historians
estimate that at least 2.5 million East Germans
escaped to West Germany during the postwar years.

The Soviets wanted to stop people from leaving
East Germany. During the night of August 12–13,
1961, Soviet troops put up a fence made of cinder

blocks and barbed-wire fence that sealed off West Berlin from the rest of East Germany. The barbed wire was gradually replaced with a concrete wall.

The Berlin Wall surrounded West Berlin. The wall was 12 feet high (3.7 m), nearly 100 miles long (161 km), and protected by guard towers, land mines, and police dogs. Guards were authorized to shoot to kill anyone who approached the wall or tried to cross it.

West Berlin became physically trapped. It remained a tiny island of capitalism in a great communist sea for many years.

"Vivid Demonstration"

The harsh Soviet tactics of controlling their population seemed extreme to people worldwide. Visiting Berlin in 1963, President Kennedy commented, "But we have never had to put a wall up to keep our people in—to prevent them from leaving us. . . . While the wall is the most obvious and vivid demonstration of the failures of the Communist system—for all the world to see."[2]

THE VIETNAM WAR

The conflict in Vietnam started somewhat like the situation in Korea. North Vietnam was under Communist rule, with Soviet ties, and South Vietnam was a U.S. ally. The situation in South Vietnam grew unstable while John F. Kennedy was president of the United States in the early 1960s.

After Kennedy was assassinated in 1963, Lyndon Johnson became president. Johnson ordered U.S. troops into Vietnam after North Vietnamese forces attacked U.S. ships.

The Vietnam War created upheavals at home and abroad. While hundreds of thousands of young soldiers were battling to the death in the jungles of Southeast Asia, hundreds of thousands of young people in the United States were protesting in the streets. College students and other youth argued against the military draft, which selected men to become soldiers without their consent. They did not want to go to

The Bay of Pigs Invasion

In April 1961, a group of Cuban exiles trained and equipped by the U.S. Central Intelligence Agency (CIA) attempted to invade Cuba. The exiles had been forced to leave Cuba. Now, they wanted to go back to start a citizens' revolution that would overthrow Fidel Castro.

On April 17, the U.S.-backed army tried to infiltrate the island, landing ships at the Bay of Pigs on Cuba's southern coast. But Castro was ready for the attack. His own troops had been trained and were supported by the Soviet Union, which wanted to keep Cuba a Communist nation. The CIA's invasion plan failed spectacularly, due to poor planning, insufficient training, and a lack of popular support for a revolution among Cubans.

The Bay of Pigs fiasco was an embarrassment for the recently elected President Kennedy. It also intensified Castro's distrust of Americans and increased his loyalty to the Soviet Union. It thus laid the groundwork for the Cuban Missile Crisis, which would occur about 18 months later.

war to fight for a cause they did not believe in. A few even argued in favor of communism, believing that U.S. democratic capitalism was not serving its citizens as well as it could.

Social pressure at home and military struggles in the field eventually led the United States to pull out of Vietnam in 1973 without a victory. Communism appeared to be gaining the upper hand after three decades of U.S. success at containment. In the summer of 1979, a Marxist faction took over the government of Nicaragua. Then, the Soviets sent troops into Afghanistan in December 1979 to support a communist revolution in the capital, Kabul. As the 1980s began, the Soviet Union was striving to increase its influence around the world.

Ich Bin Ein Berliner

In the summer of 1963, President Kennedy toured West Berlin and visited the wall. In his remarks that day, he said, "Two thousand years ago, the proudest boast in the world was *civis Romanum sum* [I am a citizen of Rome]. Today, in the world of freedom, the proudest boast is *Ich bin ein Berliner* [I am a Berliner.]"[3] He meant that West Berlin residents should take pride in being free, since their neighbors were trapped behind the wall. He told them their struggle was being recognized and respected throughout the world.

*A Soviet post on the supply route to Russia
during the Afghanistan invasion*

The original CIA headquarters in Langley, Virginia

ESPIONAGE

uring the Cold War, both sides relied on espionage, or spying, to find out what the enemy was thinking and planning. Spies were trained to sneak behind enemy lines and pick up sensitive or classified information. Both sides deployed their best military technology to keep watch on the enemy. Leaders would then use that intelligence for their own political and military advantage.

Intelligence Agencies

The headquarters for spies in the United States was, and still is, the Central Intelligence Agency (CIA). The CIA was formed in the United States after World War II. During the war, the Office of Strategic Services (OSS) had gathered intelligence for the country. Under the threat of the Cold War, President Truman knew that covert operations needed to continue.

On July 26, the National Security Act of 1947 established the CIA as a formal government organization. The leader of the organization would be appointed by the president to oversee clandestine operations and intelligence gathering worldwide. The act also created the National Security Council to advise the president on foreign affairs and national security.

Throughout the Cold War, the CIA would gather intelligence through many different channels. It monitored radio transmissions and correspondence between Soviet states, kept reports on Soviet actions around the world, and sent spies behind the iron curtain to infiltrate Communist governments.

In the Soviet Union, the *Komitet Gosudarstvennoy Bezopasnosti*, or KGB, was responsible for intelligence gathering throughout the Cold War. Established in March 1954, the KGB operated from inside the Kremlin—the fortress in the capital, Moscow, where the Soviet government met. KGB agents performed a similar function for the Soviet Union as their CIA counterparts did for the United States. Both sides worked on elaborate strategies and tried to keep one step ahead of the other.

On the U.S. home front, the Federal Bureau of Investigations (FBI) tracked down suspected traitors and spies. The FBI had been in existence much longer than the CIA, and the two agencies sometimes clashed over jurisdiction, or decisions about who controlled what areas of intelligence and covert action.

Spy Equipment

Visitors to the International Spy Museum in Washington DC can get a firsthand glimpse of some of the inventions that Cold War-era spies used. These include a lipstick gun, a fountain pen gun, encryption devices and code-breaking machines, and recording devices such as bugs and wires.

Spies Everywhere

On both sides of the iron curtain, countless individuals risked their lives trying to obtain intelligence to help their government win the Cold War. Most of their names remain locked in classified files deep in the CIA headquarters or the Kremlin. It is likely that a lot of the decisions made by world leaders at the time were based on information brought by their spies. A lot of these agents died unknown or unclaimed by their governments.

The emphasis on spies made it difficult for governments to trust even their own citizens. Loyalty was prized but difficult to prove. Throughout the Cold War era, several high profile espionage cases came to trial in the United States. Citizens were accused of passing information to the Soviets. Among the first and most famous examples was the case of Alger Hiss, a former U.S. State Department employee accused of sharing state secrets with the Soviets. The Hiss trial was very big news in 1949 because Hiss had been a well-respected public figure. The situation frightened a

The Alger Hiss Case

Alger Hiss was president of the Carnegie Endowment for International Peace, a prestigious charitable organization, when he was accused of being a Soviet spy by Whittaker Chambers, a former Communist. Hiss had once worked at the U.S. State Department, where he had access to secret documents.

Hiss managed to escape the charges at first, but Chambers later showed microfilms of documents typed on Hiss's typewriter that proved that Hiss knew more than he had admitted. Hiss was convicted of perjury in 1950 because he had lied in his first trial. He was never convicted of espionage. Hiss never admitted any wrongdoing, but more evidence revealed after the Cold War made it very likely he was involved in spying.

lot of people because it made communism seem insidious—like it could appear suddenly where it was not expected.

TECHNOLOGICAL ESPIONAGE

In addition to sending humans behind enemy lines, the United States and the Soviet Union both developed technologies for intelligence gathering. One advantage to using electronic "spies" was that they were sure to be loyal. Another was that they presented unfiltered information with little chance of human error. In other words, the governments did not have to worry if the machines were secretly working for the other side, if the information could be trusted, or if it was accurate.

The United States developed its U-2 spy planes in the mid-1950s. The U-2s could take clear pictures of the ground while flying higher than Soviet surface-to-air missiles could reach. In other words, the Soviets

Shot Down

On May 1, 1960, a U-2 spy plane was shot down over the Soviet Union. President Eisenhower told Soviets—and Americans—a weather aircraft had wandered off course. He denied that the United States was trying to spy on the Soviet Union. But pilot Francis Gary Powers survived the crash, and Premier Khrushchev announced that the Soviets had recovered the pilot and the plane. Eisenhower was forced to admit that he had lied.

Powers was sentenced to ten years in a Soviet prison. After serving two years, he was released to the United States in exchange for Soviet spy Rudolf Abel.

would be able to see the spy planes but would not be able to shoot them down. This gave the United States a huge advantage. Within four years, though, the Soviets had developed better antiaircraft missiles, putting the U-2 planes at risk.

In October 1957, the Soviet Union launched Sputnik, the first human-made satellite, into Earth's orbit. Satellites could photograph Earth and locate military bases and ships. Both the satellite and the Soviet's advanced missile technology alarmed Americans.

HOUSE UN-AMERICAN ACTIVITIES COMMITTEE

The House Un-American Activities Committee

Traitors: Julius and Ethel Rosenberg

In the summer of 1950, the FBI arrested Julius Rosenberg and his wife, Ethel. The couple was accused of being part of a spy ring that had passed atomic bomb secrets to the Soviet Union. In 1951, the Rosenbergs were tried for espionage in New York City. They were sentenced to death.

Many Americans were convinced that the charges against the couple were false, but many others were sure they had been spies. Julius and Ethel Rosenberg were executed by electric chair at Sing Sing prison in New York State on June 19, 1953. Despite the initial controversy, it is now believed that the Rosenbergs were in fact passing critical intelligence information to the Soviets.

Ethel Rosenberg was only the second woman ever to be executed for a federal crime in the United States. The first was Mary Surratt, who was hanged in 1865 for her part in Abraham Lincoln's assassination. The Rosenbergs were the first U.S. traitors executed during peacetime.

(HUAC) began as the Select Committee on Un-American Activities in 1938, a special investigative committee that looked for Americans who might be involved in Communist activities. Congress empowered HUAC to hunt for "red," or Communist, supporters. HUAC quickly expanded its scope from government employees to all Americans. HUAC was formally established as a permanent House committee in 1945.

As the game of espionage continued, the U.S. government began to fear the presence of spies within its borders. In the late 1940s, President Truman began requiring government workers to take oaths of loyalty to the United States. He wanted to rule out the possibility that there might be Soviet spies in the CIA, the White House, the Pentagon, or elsewhere in the high reaches of government. A large part of the next decade was spent searching for traitors among the U.S. citizenry.

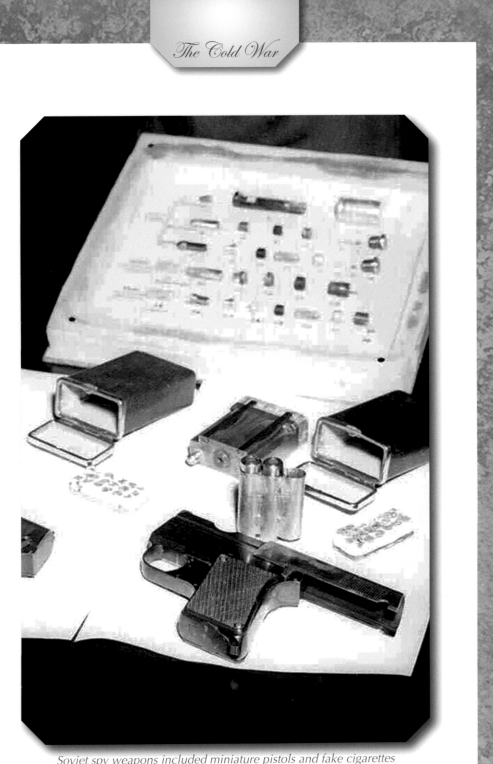

Soviet spy weapons included miniature pistols and fake cigarettes
that shot poisonous bullets.

Senator Joseph McCarthy's tactics contributed to the hysteria over communism in the United States.

THE RED SCARE

The U.S. government's fear of Soviet spies made life in the United States a challenge for many people. HUAC and its investigations led to public hysteria over Communist spies who they feared might be living in the United States.

The U.S. Constitution protects people's rights to political freedom. Thus, the Communist Party was free to exist in the United States, and it had a healthy membership. The party had gained popularity in the 1930s during the Great Depression.

After World War II, members of the Communist Party automatically fell under suspicion. Anticommunists targeted known members of the party, their friends and colleagues, and anyone who had ever attended a Communist Party meeting or rally. Communists and people who sympathized with them quickly learned to hide their interest in politics.

McCarthyism and Hysteria

The Cold War–era hunt for Communists is often referred to as McCarthyism, after the leader of the anticommunist hysteria, Wisconsin

The First Red Scare

The Red Scare of the 1940s and 1950s was actually the second instance of anticommunist hysteria in the United States. The first Red Scare happened from 1917 to 1920, during and after World War I (1914–1918). After the Bolshevik Revolution occurred in Russia in 1917, a new, Communist government formed there, led by Vladimir Lenin. Americans were frightened that the United States would be threatened by the Communists.

Loyalty Oath

During the Red Scare, citizens were commonly required to prove their loyalty to the United States. Many states put sedition laws in place—laws that would punish traitors. Twenty-five states, Washington DC, Puerto Rico, and Alaska (which became a state in 1959) required teachers to take oaths of allegiance, stating that they were loyal to the United States, had no affiliation to the Communist Party, and would not teach Communist principles to their students.

Senator Joseph R. McCarthy. Senator McCarthy believed that Communist spies were everywhere, hiding among ordinary citizens. Both McCarthy's Senate committee and HUAC called thousands of witnesses to testify about Communist activities. Citizens were encouraged to report the names of any Communists they knew.

While some people immediately cooperated with HUAC and McCarthy investigations, others were outraged at the committees' actions. The committees' questions about people's political party affiliations and personal beliefs went against the First Amendment rights to freedom of speech and assembly outlined in the U.S. Constitution. Some people refused to testify on this basis. The hysteria was so strong, however, that the committees tried to demonize anyone who stood silent under the First Amendment.

BLACKLISTING

As the Red Scare grew stronger, certain groups of people fell under suspicion right away. Artists, actors, Hollywood screenwriters, directors and producers, authors, union workers, professionals such as doctors and lawyers, and Jewish people were frequently accused. Quite a few of these people were well known in their fields. When the spotlight was cast on them, it sometimes ruined their careers, even if they were found innocent.

On November 24, 1947, a group of ten Hollywood writers and directors refused to testify when they were called before HUAC. The ten were cited in contempt of court for refusing to cooperate. That night, members of the Association of Motion Picture Producers, including influential studio officials, came together and released the Waldorf Declaration, firing those

Witch Hunt

Some historians compare the Red Scare and the Cold War anticommunist hysteria with the witch hunts of the sixteenth and seventeenth centuries. These hunts for men and women accused of witchcraft, similar to the Red Scare, were fed by mass hysteria and social pressure to get rid of undesirable members of the community.

Today, some people compare the Red Scare to the fear of terrorists—while the threat is real, sometimes citizens and governments allow themselves to look too hard for potential threats, and end up blaming some innocent people along the way.

ten individuals and refusing to hire anyone having anything to do with communism. That was the beginning of the entertainment industry blacklist.

Today, the term *blacklist* is sometimes casually used to refer to someone who cannot get a job in a certain industry for social or political reasons. In the early 1950s, the blacklists caused serious problems for many innocent people. In some cases, suspected Communists automatically ended up on blacklists. People who refused to cooperate with HUAC or declined to name names to the committee were blacklisted, too.

Many innocent people were called to testify, and when they could not provide helpful information, the accusations against them grew stronger. If those accused could not disprove their association with the Communist Party, they might be barred from certain jobs.

Blacklisted

Some famous people who were added to the black-list include:

• Leonard Bernstein, the composer of the musical *West Side Story*

• Langston Hughes, author and poet

• Arthur Miller, author of the plays *Death of a Salesman* and *The Crucible*

• Orson Welles, the star and director of the film *Citizen Kane*

Hollywood director Edward Dmytryk is questioned at a HUAC hearing in 1951.

They could be required to identify their communist friends to HUAC. Blacklists were just one way people who were suspected of being Communists faced challenges beyond the courtroom. Friends and neighbors often shied away from accused Communists, even if they knew the charges were false. They did not want to be accused of being Communist, too.

Citizen Readiness

The Red Scare increased fear across the country, while the threat of nuclear war still interrupted Americans' daily lives. People were afraid of spies in their midst, Communists, and war. There was little that average citizens could do to protect themselves.

The Federal Civil Defense Administration provided information to help citizens protect themselves in the event of a nuclear incident. The information campaign was targeted to suburban areas. It was believed that any nuclear attack from the Soviet Union would be aimed at cities. Residents of a city hit by a bomb would almost certainly be killed in the blast, so residents of the suburbs would have the best chance of survival.

At school, children practiced air-raid drills the way students today practice fire drills. As a warning siren went off, all students were supposed to drop to the floor, crawl under their desks, and cover their heads with their arms. In reality, these measures would not have prevented damage from a nuclear blast. People built fallout shelters in their backyards. Most of these shelters were poorly built and would not have truly protected their occupants. The drills and shelters were intended to make citizens feel safer—as if there was something they could do. The real effect of these measures was quite the opposite. They constantly reminded people of the threat of war and made people edgy with worry. Media coverage of events such as the Cuban Missile Crisis had many Americans worried that nuclear war was about to begin.

Fortunately, the fear of nuclear war lost some of its intensity over time. U.S. involvement in the Korean War, the Vietnam War, and the growing

Fallout Shelters

Many families built bomb shelters in their basements or backyards. The shelters were typically built of concrete or buried in the earth. The purpose of the shelters was to protect people from harmful radiation from nuclear fallout. In most cases, individual family shelters probably had significant safety flaws. If they were not built of the right materials in the right way, people could suffocate, overheat, or end up affected by radiation anyway.

A typical fallout shelter would contain some or all of the following: several weeks' supply of canned food and bottled or canned water; flashlights; lanterns; a battery-powered radio; ventilation system with radiation filters; electrical generator; sleeping bags and mattresses or cots; a chemical toilet or waste disposal system; a Geiger counter for measuring radioactive particles in the air; a first-aid kit; guns for protection; and personal items such as books, clothing, and toys.

civil rights movement gave people other things to think and worry about. The Cold War was by no means over, but people settled into believing that it really was a *cold* war. ⌁

*A family-type bomb shelter made in 1958
could hold eight to twelve people.*

The "Fat Man" type of atomic bomb was used in 1945.

New Technology

or most Americans, the Red Scare was related to the fear of nuclear war. The nuclear threat hung like a shadow over the world. It began the moment the United States dropped atomic bombs on Hiroshima and Nagasaki at the end of World War II. Everything world leaders knew about warfare had changed.

BUILDING BOMBS

When the atomic bombs were dropped on Japan in August 1945, nuclear technology was a new science. Only seven years earlier, German scientists split a uranium atom. Their discovery led researchers in the United States to develop the first atomic bomb. These workers were on the cutting edge of their field. Some of the greatest scientific and mathematical minds of the twentieth century contributed ideas to the effort. Researchers were excited by the possibilities of nuclear technology, but they were also afraid of it. They knew these weapons would be more destructive than anything the world had ever seen.

In 1939, physicist Albert Einstein wrote a letter to President Franklin

Nuclear Technology

There are two types of nuclear reactions used to build bombs: fission and fusion. Atomic bombs are fission bombs. The nucleus of one atom is split, which creates a huge burst of energy. Then the pieces of the first atom fly around splitting other atoms, creating more energy. Hydrogen bombs are fusion bombs. The nucleus of one atom is forced to bond with another, which creates an even larger initial burst of energy than fission does. This begins a chain reaction of similar bursts.

A Terrible Thing

Atomic and nuclear technology has never been taken lightly. The scientists who created these weapons and the politicians who have been charged with deciding on their use respect and fear these bombs' power. President Truman once told his advisers, "It is a terrible thing to order the use of something that . . . is so terribly destructive, destructive beyond anything we have ever had. . . . So we have got to treat this differently from rifles and cannon and ordinary things like that."[1]

Truman's successor, President Eisenhower, later said, "If the Kremlin and Washington ever lock up in a war, the results are too horrible to contemplate."[2]

D. Roosevelt warning him that scientific research could lead to a powerful new kind of weapon. Einstein and his colleagues were concerned about the Germans working on such a bomb. Roosevelt took the threat seriously. When the United States entered World War II, he brought a team of scientists together to work on the bomb for the U.S. military. Based in a secret facility in Los Alamos, New Mexico, the research effort was called the Manhattan Project.

The Manhattan Project scientists developed the first atomic bomb using a radioactive element called uranium. The theory of creating nuclear reactions in uranium was easy. The challenge was figuring out how to control these nuclear reactions and inserting them into devices that would explode when and how the scientists wanted them to. The process took several years. They tested the first bomb in the New Mexico desert in July 1945.

Albert Einstein's letter to President Franklin D. Roosevelt led to the creation of the Manhattan Project.

THE ARMS RACE

In the hostile Cold War climate, the Soviet Union could not allow the United States sole control of the most powerful weapon ever known. The Soviet Union hurried to complete the development of an atomic bomb of its own, aided by secret Manhattan Project documents that their spies had smuggled from the United States. They ran their first nuclear test on August 29, 1949.

The United States needed to keep its advantage over the Soviet Union. U.S. scientists started building a more destructive weapon, the hydrogen bomb. The Soviets, too, began working on hydrogen bombs. Both nations hoped never to use these weapons, but neither could feel secure if the other country had better weapons.

The U.S. military tested the first hydrogen bomb on November 1, 1952, on a Pacific island. The devastation was even more extensive than had been expected. The Soviet government announced that it had hydrogen bomb technology soon after, in August 1953. In August 1957, the Soviets launched the first intercontinental ballistic missile (ICBM). ICBMs allowed the Soviets to launch rockets from their own land and aim them at the United States. No planes or troops would be necessary to cause massive destruction.

The United States tested the first hydrogen bomb
in the Marshall Islands on November 1, 1952.

The arms race that ensued followed a peculiar
logic. Neither nation wanted to use the bombs, but
they kept building them. The purpose, for both
sides, was to ensure that they used diplomacy to
solve the conflict. They figured whoever had more

weapons would have a stronger position in global negotiations. They each wanted to be able to threaten the other. They did not actually want to take violent action against each other. The precarious balance was based on mutual distrust.

THE SPACE RACE

In 1961, President John F. Kennedy stepped into office with a new vision for the country. Americans needed to be freed of fear of nuclear war. They needed to be inspired. They needed to be assured of the country's status as a superpower. In an address before Congress in May 1961, Kennedy laid out his priorities for the country. He announced that he would make it the goal of his administration to land an American on the moon before the end of the decade.

People were stunned. They did not believe it possible—nothing even

The Apollo Program

Neil Armstrong and Buzz Aldrin were part of the successful Apollo 11 moon landing mission, but this mission was just one of a series of space explorations between 1963 and 1972. Other notable missions included Apollo 10, which orbited the moon, and Apollos 12–17, which were also moon landing missions. Apollo 13, which was intended as a moon landing, was called back due to a catastrophic technical failure that nearly killed all three astronauts on board.

remotely close had ever been attempted. It would cost a lot of money and take a lot of time. It would require great risks. But still, the idea captured the country's imagination.

Kennedy's announcement was not just a flight of fancy. The Soviets were ahead in the space race. They had launched Sputnik in 1957. The Soviets had just sent the first human into space in April 1961. The United States needed to compete with the Soviets to be on the cutting edge of every industry,

Everyday Technology

The National Aeronautics and Space Administration (NASA) space program created some technologies that we use every day, including cordless appliances, sports-equipment padding, and better communications.

The space program pushed for innovation in battery-powered tools. Such tools existed previously, but NASA's needs for better tools for astronauts in space propelled the industry to make improvements. One result of better technology was a cordless, handheld vacuum, often called a Dust Buster. Astronauts also needed wireless communication systems in their helmets so they could stay in contact with mission control. Today, the next generation of this technology is seen in wireless headsets for cell phones and video games.

NASA developed a material to cushion aircraft seats—the same material is used today in baseball helmets and football pads. Today, other NASA materials make invisible braces, athletic shoes, and scratch-resistant sunglasses.

Satellites have had a huge impact on modern communications. The first satellites were sent into orbit to gather information about space. Soon, satellites allowed people on the ground to communicate with those in space. Quickly, the technology began to improve communication on Earth, too. Today, satellites bounce signals around the planet, allowing us to communicate by phone, Internet, and television.

not just nuclear arms. On July 20, 1969, Kennedy's goal was achieved when Americans Neil Armstrong and Edwin "Buzz" Aldrin became the first humans to walk on the moon. ⌐

"For the eyes of the world now look into space, to the moon and to the planets beyond, and we have vowed that we shall not see it governed by a hostile flag of conquest, but by a banner of freedom and peace. We have vowed that we shall not see space filled with weapons of mass destruction, but with instruments of knowledge and understanding.

"Yet the vows of this Nation can only be fulfilled if we in this Nation are first, and, therefore, we intend to be first. In short, our leadership in science and in industry, our hopes for peace and security, our obligations to ourselves as well as others, all require us to make this effort, to solve these mysteries, to solve them for the good of all men, and to become the world's leading space-faring nation."[3]

—*President Kennedy, September 12, 1962*

Astronaut Edwin "Buzz" Aldrin stands by the U.S. flag
on the moon on July 20, 1969.

The preliminary SALT agreement was signed on October 3, 1972.

EASING TENSIONS

For years, the United States and the Soviet Union were locked in a nuclear standoff. Both sides kept nuclear warheads aimed at the other so they could retaliate if the other side fired first. This standoff was known as mutual assured destruction, or MAD, because each country knew that if it started a nuclear war, both countries and possibly the world would be destroyed. Fortunately, neither side ever struck.

Nuclear Nonproliferation Treaty

On July 1, 1969, President Richard Nixon signed a nuclear nonproliferation treaty with the Soviet Union. It was a huge step toward calming the Cold War nuclear threat because it sought to limit the number of countries that possessed nuclear weapons.

Nixon took a great many steps toward détente, or a calming of tension, with the Soviets. Détente and the goal of nuclear nonproliferation occupied U.S. and Soviet leaders throughout the 1970s. Both nations had already built enough nuclear weapons to destroy the world a few times over, but each had kept building its stores. At this time, both countries wanted to calm the arms race. The two countries realized that excessive defense and weapons spending could hurt their economies. Neither wanted nuclear war. The 1969 treaty opened the door for a series of Strategic Arms Limitation Talks (SALT) that began in 1970. By 1972, the talks resulted in two new arms agreements. SALT was considered a temporary

On January 16, 1984, President Reagan gave a speech in which he invited the possibility of negotiation with the Soviets. He said:

"Just suppose with me for a moment that an Ivan and an Anya [Russians] could find themselves, say, in a waiting room, or sharing a shelter from the rain or a storm with a Jim and Sally [Americans], and that there was no language barrier to keep them from getting acquainted. Would they then deliberate the differences between their respective governments? Or would they find themselves comparing notes about their children and what each other did for a living? . . . They might even have decided that they were all going to get together for dinner some evening soon. Above all, they would have proven that people don't make wars."[1]

agreement, however. The two countries lacked a permanent treaty.

After President Nixon resigned from office in August 1974, President Gerald Ford and later President Jimmy Carter picked up the arms negotiations. They reached several more treaties and agreements with the Soviets, but tensions remained.

The second round of Strategic Arms Limitation Talks (SALT II) were signed in 1979. SALT II was intended to be a more permanent and complete treaty than the first SALT agreements. The difficult negotiations lasted about six years and ended with an agreement that did not satisfy either side. The agreements were never implemented.

Power Shifts

Between 1978 and 1980, a series of dramatic confrontations in the Middle East upset the Cold War balance once again. In 1979,

when a Marxist faction took over
the government in Afghanistan, the
Soviet Union quickly sent troops
to Afghanistan to support the new
regime. Communism was not very
popular in Afghanistan, and the
Soviets feared the new leaders might
be overthrown.

Also in 1979, a pro-American
government in Iran was overthrown.
The United States had supported
the Iranian government because
it was anticommunist, but Iranian
citizens were unhappy with their
leader's harsh style. The new leader,
Ayatollah Khomeini, established a
strictly Islamic government. Even
though Iran had not turned toward
communism, the United States had
lost an ally in the Middle East.

In 1981, a workers' uprising in
Poland threatened Soviet Communist
rule. The Soviet army was busy in
Afghanistan, and Soviet leaders
had to decide whether to fight the

Poland

Poland was a satellite
state of the Soviet Union.
Under its Communist
government, elections
were controlled by the
party, and the people
lacked freedom of speech
and other rights. Throughout the Cold War era,
various groups staged
protests and uprisings
against the Communist
government. Finally, in
1989, the Polish people
gained the right to free
elections and reformed
their government.

Ayatollah Khomeini became the leader of Iran in 1979.

revolution in Poland. In the end, they did not
intervene, which showed the world that the Soviets'
military might was not what it once had been. The
Polish government restored control itself.

REAGAN AND GORBACHEV

In 1981, Ronald Reagan became president of the United States. When he took office, Reagan was staunchly anticommunist. He did not trust the Soviet Union and began increasing the size of the military. However, in 1985, Mikhail Gorbachev took power in the Soviet Union. Reagan and Gorbachev began negotiations. The two leaders grew to trust and understand each other, and diplomacy improved.

Within the Soviet Union, Gorbachev began a series of reforms intended to improve the peoples' standard of living. He followed two policies, *glasnost* (openness) and *perestroika* (restructuring). Glasnost called for less secrecy in the Soviet government. Perestroika encouraged economic and political reform.

The global situation indicated that the Soviet Union might not be able to hold onto its power much longer. Reagan wanted to end the Cold War. He was determined that the United States and the Soviet Union could come to an agreement that would serve them both and free the world of the tension between the superpowers, albeit with the United States in a stronger position. Gorbachev knew that the Soviet Union could not keep up in the arms race with the United States. He had to compromise to try to save his country's economy.

THE WALL WILL FALL

In 1987 in Berlin, President Reagan demanded, "Mr. Gorbachev, tear down this wall!"[2] By 1989, George H. W. Bush was the U.S. president, and the Soviet Union was in distress. Its economy was falling apart, and Gorbachev's policies of glasnost and perestroika encouraged the satellite states to demand democratic reforms. Authorities in Moscow were quickly losing control of their satellite states.

Strategic Defense Initiative

President Reagan challenged the standoff mentality of the nuclear arms race when he introduced the Strategic Defense Initiative (SDI). If the country were ever attacked by nuclear weapons, Reagan wanted to be able to defend against them. U.S. military scientists set to work developing a defense system that would prevent launched nuclear weapons from reaching their target. In the long term, Reagan hoped to make nuclear weapons useless. If any fired nuclear warhead could be intercepted and destroyed, there would be no point in firing it. In the short term, being the first to have this kind of technology would have given the United States the upper hand in any military situation. Reagan believed it could end the Cold War.

Reagan announced the idea for SDI in a nationally televised speech on March 23, 1983. It excited some Americans and frightened the Soviets, who had no such technology in the works yet. The Soviets feared that SDI was already operational, or close. The SDI was nowhere near ready, but Reagan had successfully made the point he wanted to make.

Successful uprisings in Poland, Hungary, and Romania were followed by dissension in East Germany. East German citizens began flooding into Czechoslovakia and Hungary. From there, they could escape across the Austrian border into free territory. Several thousand East Germans climbed the fence of West Germany's embassy in Prague, Czechoslovakia, seeking asylum and transport to West Germany.

"Nothing Is Eternal"

In June 1989, a German reporter asked Gorbachev if the Berlin Wall would ever come down. Mr. Gorbachev responded: "Nothing is eternal in this world."[3] Less than six months later, the wall was torn down.

The East German government was embarrassed by the flood of people trying to leave the country. It was a sign that the Communist government had failed. On November 9, 1989, the East German government decided to relax the rules about crossing through the Berlin Wall. They thought this would appease unhappy citizens. The relaxed rules did not have the desired effect. As soon as word came through that the wall was open, thousands of people crossed, overwhelming the guards.

Pieces of the Wall

The night the East Germans relaxed their guard at the wall, the citizens of Berlin rejoiced. Huge crowds descended on the wall and literally tore it down, chipping away piece by piece with bare hands and whatever tools they had. Many kept pieces of the wall as souvenirs. For some, that night was a reunion with family members and friends they had not seen in 28 years.

Most of the wall still stood physically after that night, but the symbolic meaning of its opening could never be taken back. ⌣

Berliners help one another cross the Berlin Wall after the border of
East and West Germany is opened.

Protestors gather outside the Kremlin in opposition to communism on February 4, 1990.

THE AFTERMATH

he fall of the Berlin Wall was symbolic of the fall of communism. Shortly after that historic event, the Soviet Union itself would collapse. The Cold War was all but over. Even though the fall of the Berlin Wall was a sign of the Cold War's end, it

was not the true end. As had been the case following
World War II, Soviet and U.S. leaders debated—this
time with the Germans—about what to do with
Germany. East Germany was part of the Warsaw Pact,
while West Germany was part of NATO. After much
negotiation, the leaders agreed to allow Germany
to reunite as a member of NATO and to allow U.S.
troops to remain in the country to help keep order.
The Soviet Union withdrew its forces from East
Berlin and East Germany, and the two halves of the
country reunited. Many East Germans were happy to
be separated from the Soviet Union. On October 3,
1990, Germany became one nation again.

THE END OF THE SOVIET UNION

The smaller Soviet satellite states had watched
the Soviet government stand by while Poland rid
itself of communism and Germany reunified. These
small states began to think that they would have less
to fear if they showed a wish for independence,
too. By 1989, the Soviet Union had lost much of
its influence in Eastern Europe, and many of the
satellite states had gained control of their own
governments. In addition, the Soviet government
was beginning to lose control over the individual

George H. W. Bush

George H. W. Bush was born in Milton, Massachusetts on June 12, 1924. At age 18, Bush enlisted, and he soon became the youngest pilot in the navy. He flew 58 missions in the Pacific during World War II. He served two terms as a congressman representing Texas.

Bush served as the director of the CIA under President Gerald Ford. He served as vice president under Ronald Reagan and was elected president in 1988. His close relationship with Soviet leader Mikhail Gorbachev is considered a significant factor in bringing about the diplomatic and relatively peaceful end of the Cold War.

republics that made up the Soviet Union.

The Soviet experiment in imperial communism—trying to force its spread around the world—had failed. Mikhail Gorbachev recognized that failure was unavoidable, and he allowed the collapse of his homeland to happen. He held diplomatic talks with Reagan's vice president, George H. W. Bush, and they continued that relationship once Bush became president in 1988. These talks contributed to the peaceful ending of the Cold War. Gorbachev won the Nobel Peace Prize in 1990 for this great achievement.

Gorbachev was a committed Communist, but he was wise enough to see that much of the world did not accept the Soviet agenda. He could have sent the Soviet army to force the issue, as his predecessors had done. However, he wanted peace. Gorbachev's last act in office was to

Mikhail Gorbachev ended the Cold War and dissolved the Soviet Union.

officially disband the Soviet Union. He signed the
document on Christmas Day, December 25, 1991.
The Soviet Union dissolved on December 31, and
the Soviet republics became independent countries.

NEW ALLIES AND ENEMIES

The end of the Cold War allowed states that had stood against one another to become allies. The Warsaw Pact between the Soviet Union and its satellite states dissolved, and those nations became free to join NATO. The United States and the newly formed nation of Russia also began a slow, tentative alliance.

The United States celebrated the collapse of the Soviet Union and the fall of imperial communism as a national victory. U.S. leaders quickly turned to helping the new Russian government rebuild itself and become part of the democratic international community.

Without the Soviet Union as its archenemy, the United States had to change its outlook on the world. The situation was no longer black and white, capitalist and Communist. Communism still existed in places around the world, but it was no

Soviet Successor States

The Soviet Union broke up into its republics, including the very large Russian Federation (Russia) and smaller chunks that became the following countries: Belarus, Ukraine, Moldova, Georgia, Armenia, Azerbaijan, Uzbekistan, Kazakhstan, Turkmenistan, Kyrgyzstan, Tajikistan, Estonia, Latvia, and Lithuania.

longer backed by the economic and military might
of the Soviet Union. Small nations no longer had to
choose between the Americans or the Soviets. The
choice was now up to these small nations over how
they would govern themselves. New revolutionary
groups cropped up, with radical political ideals,
a strong thirst for power, or fanatical religious
convictions. The Cold War was over, but the world's
conflicts were not.

TWENTY YEARS LATER

Many years have
passed since the
fall of the Berlin
Wall and the end
of the Cold War.
However, the
world still feels the
effects of that long
conflict. The U.S.
and Soviet efforts
to spread their
beliefs around the
globe left many

Cold War Legacies

The Cold War was a long, sustained conflict
that intersected with at least ten different U.S.
presidencies:

Franklin D. Roosevelt—Allied with Soviets
during WWII, initiated the Manhattan Project

Harry S. Truman—Ordered the bombing of
Hiroshima and Nagasaki, Truman Doctrine,
Berlin Blockade, NATO, Korean War

Dwight D. Eisenhower—Korean War

John F. Kennedy—Set the goal of sending an
American to the moon, Cuban Missile Crisis,
Vietnam War

Lyndon B. Johnson—Vietnam War

Richard M. Nixon—Vietnam War, SALT I
talks and treaty

Gerald Ford—SALT II talks

Jimmy Carter—SALT II talks and failed treaty

Ronald Reagan—Increased arms production, diplomacy to end the Cold War

George H. W. Bush—End of the Cold War

A ceremonial wall was toppled in Berlin during the twentieth anniversary of the fall of the Berlin Wall.

aftereffects. Even though people refer to "the fall of communism" when they talk about the collapse of the Soviet Union, there are still Communist nations in the world today. North Korea, Vietnam, Cuba, China, and Laos are such states.

The U.S. Communist Party has recovered from the McCarthy-era Red Scare, too. Today, the party members are again free to meet and declare their beliefs.

Nuclear Proliferation

The weapons developed during the Cold War are still the deadliest the world has ever known. It is fortunate that the hydrogen bomb has never been used in warfare. The nuclear threat still exists, even though the Cold War is over.

Producing nuclear bombs is very expensive. For decades, it would have been impossible for any small nation or group to manage bomb production. That is no longer the case, and this gives rise to a number of new concerns. What if someone outside the nonproliferation treaty gets access to nuclear technology? Should the superpowers of the world have a right to defend themselves in the face of terror, or an unforeseen enemy that may arise?

Moreover, there is the possibility that small groups, usually referred to as terrorists, may gain access to nuclear bombs. These groups are not interested in diplomacy, and they usually do not represent any state or country. They are out for

The Nuclear Threat Continues

As of 2010, nine nations in the world held a total of approximately 22,000 nuclear weapons among them. Two more countries had tested nuclear explosives or were suspected of having them. World opinion is that these weapons are unlikely to be used by these powers, except in an extreme case of self-defense, but it is widely believed that their presence is a threat to security anyway.

In 2005, Nobel Peace Prize recipient and Director General of the International Atomic Energy Agency Mohamed ElBaradei said, "I have no doubt that, if we hope to escape self-destruction, then nuclear weapons should have no place in our collective conscience, and no role in our security."[1]

their own interests and accountable to no one, which makes them very dangerous.

The United States fears the presence of weapons of mass destruction—nuclear and other weapons that can kill large numbers of people—in the hands of leaders who do not ally with U.S. interests and may not be interested in international diplomacy. In 2009, the United States met with North Korea over these issues. Still a Communist state, North Korea has sustained a tense relationship with the United States over the years.

Political instability in the Middle East and the continued desire to protect U.S. interests abroad led the U.S. government to send troops to Iraq, Afghanistan, and other locations in recent decades. Though the "enemy" there is no longer communism, U.S. leaders still claim a desire to promote democracy and support fledgling democratic governments. U.S. diplomats also began talks with Iran about its nuclear ambitions.

THE COLD WAR LEGACY

After decades of tension, competition, and fears of nuclear war, the end of the Cold War was a relief to the world. However, the era's effects are still felt everywhere. Many historians believe that the United States is in a more complicated global conflict today than it ever was during the Cold War era. Back then, the Soviet Union was the only opposition, and the spread of communism was the greatest threat. The nuclear threat was really just a diplomatic standoff, and both sides desperately worked to keep it that way.

Today, the threat of nuclear war continues. Small countries, militant revolutionaries, and rogue political and religious organizations are beginning to build or obtain the destructive weapons. Thus, a Cold War technology that was designed to keep the world safe became a great danger.

The Cold War succeeded in uniting Americans and strengthening the nation's vision for itself and the entire world. Mistakes were made, victories were won, and losses were felt, but Americans look back on this time as one of the formative eras of their republic. With good reason, the Cold War conflict between the United States and the Soviet Union is remembered as one of the most significant conflicts in history. ⌐

*Gorbachev, left, and Bush signing treaties that contributed
to the end of the Cold War, June 1, 1990*

TIMELINE

1848	**1917**	**1946**
The Communist Manifesto is published in London.	Vladimir Lenin leads the Bolshevik Revolution, which leads to the forming of the USSR.	Winston Churchill delivers his "Iron Curtain" speech in Fulton, Missouri, on March 5.

1949	**1949**	**1950**
The North Atlantic Treaty Organization is formed on April 4.	The Soviet blockade of West Berlin ends on May 12.	North Korean troops invade South Korea on June 24, sparking U.S. involvement in the Korean War until 1953.

1947

The Marshall Plan to bolster economic recovery in Europe is announced on June 5.

1947

The National Security Act establishes the CIA and the National Security Council on July 26.

1948

The Soviets blockade West Berlin on June 24.

1952

The United States tests the first hydrogen bomb on November 1.

1955

The Soviet Union and its allies sign the Warsaw Pact in Poland in May.

1957

The Soviet Union launches Sputnik in October.

TIMELINE

1961

The United States sends troops to aid the government in Vietnam. The troops will remain until 1973.

1961

The U.S.-led Bay of Pigs Invasion in Cuba fails on April 17.

1961

President Kennedy announces on May 25 that he wants to land an astronaut on the moon before the end of the decade.

1970

Strategic Arms Limitation Talks begin between U.S. and Soviet leaders.

1979

Soviet troops invade Afghanistan in December.

1983

President Reagan announces the Strategic Defense Initiative on March 23.

1961	1962	1969
The Soviets erect the Berlin Wall on August 12–13.	For two tense weeks, the Cuban Missile Crisis takes center stage in world politics.	Apollo 11 astronauts walk on the moon on July 20.

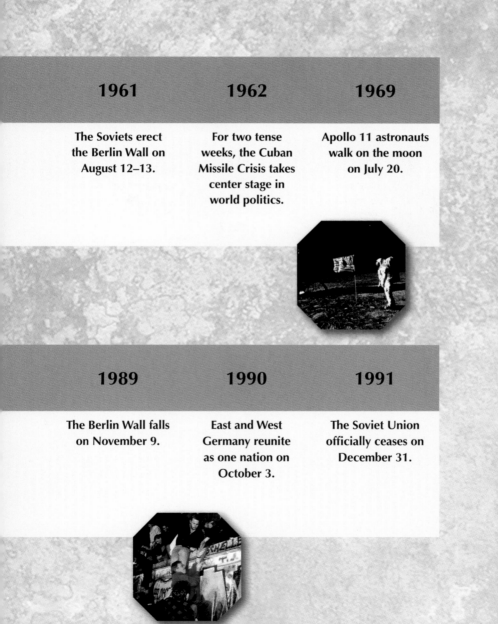

1989	1990	1991
The Berlin Wall falls on November 9.	East and West Germany reunite as one nation on October 3.	The Soviet Union officially ceases on December 31.

Essential Facts

Date of Event

1945–1991

Place of Event

The United States, the Soviet Union; conflicts occurred in countries around the world, including Korea, Vietnam, Cuba, and Eastern European and Middle Eastern nations.

Key Players

- Harry S. Truman
- John F. Kennedy
- Richard Nixon
- Ronald Reagan
- Nikita Khrushchev
- Mikhail Gorbachev

HIGHLIGHTS OF EVENT

❖ After World War II, tensions increased between the Soviet Union, a communist country, and the United States, a capitalist country.

❖ The era of tension from the 1940s to the 1990s is known as the Cold War. The United States and the Soviet Union never declared actual war on each other during this time.

❖ After World War II, the United States and its allies and the Soviet Union divided Germany and the city of Berlin among themselves. In 1961, the Soviet Union built the Berlin Wall to separate West Berlin from East Berlin.

❖ Conflicts worldwide related to the Cold War include the Korean War (1950–1953), the Vietnam War (1961–1973), and the Cuban Missile Crisis (1962).

❖ During the Cold War, the United States and the Soviet Union faced off in an arms race, which caused people to fear nuclear war. The two countries also raced to explore outer space.

❖ Fear of spies and traitors encouraged the Red Scare in the United States.

❖ The Berlin Wall fell in 1989. Other communist countries soon declared independence from Soviet influence.

❖ The Soviet Union dissolved in 1991.

QUOTE

"But we have never had to put a wall up to keep our people in—to prevent them from leaving us. . . . While the wall is the most obvious and vivid demonstration of the failures of the Communist system—for all the world to see."—*John F. Kennedy, on the Berlin Wall*

ADDITIONAL RESOURCES

SELECT BIBLIOGRAPHY

Cirincione, Joseph. *Bomb Scare: The History & Future of Nuclear Weapons.* New York: Columbia UP, 2007.

Gaddis, John Lewis. *The Cold War: A New History.* New York: Penguin, 2005.

LaFeber, Walter. *America, Russia, and the Cold War 1945–1984.* 10th ed. New York: Knopf, 2008.

Reeves, Thomas C. *Twentieth-Century America: A Brief History.* New York: Oxford UP, 2000.

Walker, Martin. *The Cold War: A History.* New York: Holt, 1993.

FURTHER READING

Brownell, Richard. *The Cold War.* Detroit, MI: Lucent, 2009.

Harrison, Paul. *The Cold War.* Farmington Hills, MI: Lucent, 2005.

Platt, Richard. *Spy.* New York: DK, 2009.

Schmemann, Serge. *When the Wall Came Down: The Berlin Wall and the Fall of Soviet Communism.* Boston: Kingfisher, 2007.

WEB LINKS

To learn more about the Cold War, visit ABDO Publishing Company online at **www.abdopublishing.com**. Web sites about the Cold War are featured on our Book Links page. These links are routinely monitored and updated to provide the most current information available.

PLACES TO VISIT

The International Spy Museum
800 F Street NW
Washington, DC 20004
202-393-7798
http://www.spymuseum.org/
The museum offers interactive exhibits on espionage throughout the ages, including the methods, tools, and lifestyles of spies on both sides of the Red Scare.

NSA Cryptologic Museum
9900 Colony 7 Rd
Fort Meade, MD 20755
301-688-5849
www.nsa.gov/about/cryptologic_heritage/museum/
Learn about the history of cryptology (the study of codes) and code breaking.

GLOSSARY

ally
> A country that gives support or friendship to another.

blacklist
> To ban a person from work in a certain industry.

blockade
> To forcefully close an area.

capitalism
> An economic system in which property is owned by individuals, not by the government.

coalition
> A group united by common interests.

communism
> An economic system in which property is owned collectively or by the government, not by individuals.

containment
> Preventing something from spreading beyond a certain area.

controversy
> A debate or disagreement.

détente
> A calming of tension.

diplomacy
> Communication and compromise between countries.

disarmament
> The removal of weapons.

espionage
> Spying.

exile

A person sent away from his or her country.

ideology
> A system of beliefs.

intelligence
> Information gathered, often in secret, that governments use to plan policy.

missile
> A bomb-carrying rocket.

nonproliferation
> Preventing the spread of nuclear weapons.

perjury
> Lying under oath, usually in a courtroom.

regime
> A ruling military group.

surveillance
> Watching or spying on something.

Source Notes

Chapter 1. Standoff
1. John F. Kennedy. "Radio and Television Report to the American People on the Soviet Arms Buildup in Cuba." *John F. Kennedy Presidential Library and Museum*. 22 Oct. 1962. 27 Oct. 2009 <http://www.jfklibrary.org/jfkl/cmc/j102262.htm>.
2. Joseph Cirincione. *Bomb Scare: The History and Future of Nuclear Weapons*. New York: Columbia University Press, 2007. xii.

Chapter 2. The Iron Curtain
1. Karl Marx and Friedrich Engels. "The Communist Manifesto." *The Marxists Internet Archive*. 1848. 27 Oct. 2009 <http://www.marxists. org/archive/marx/works/1848/communist-manifesto/ch01.htm>.
2. Winston Churchill. "Iron Curtain Speech." *Modern History Sourcebook*. 5 Mar. 1946. 27 Oct. 2009 <http://www.fordham.edu/ halsall/mod/churchill-iron.html>.
3. Ibid.

Chapter 3. The Truman Doctrine
1. Thomas C. Reeves. *Twentieth Century America: A Brief History*. New York: Oxford UP, 2000. 142.

Chapter 4. Military Mobilization
1. "Dwight D. Eisenhower." *White House Online*. 27 Oct. 2009 <http://www.whitehouse.gov/about/presidents/dwightdeisenhower/>.
2. John F. Kennedy. "Ich bin ein Berliner." *American Rhetoric Online*. 26 June 1963. 31 May 2010 <http://www.americanrhetoric.com/speeches/jfkberliner.html>.
3. Ibid.

Chapter 5. Espionage
None

Chapter 6. The Red Scare
None

Chapter 7. New Technology
1. John Lewis Gaddis. *The Cold War: A New History*. New York: Penguin, 2005. 53.
2. Ibid. 66.
3. John F. Kennedy. "Address at Rice University on the Nation's Space Program." *American Rhetoric Online*. 12 Sept. 1962. 18 June 2010 <http://www.americanrhetoric.com/speeches/jfkriceuniversity.htm>.

Source Notes Continued

Chapter 8. Easing Tensions

1. John Lewis Gaddis. *The Cold War: A New History*. New York: Penguin, 2005. 2.

2. Ronald Reagan. "Remarks at the Brandenburg Gate." *American Rhetoric Online*. 12 June 1987. 31 May 2010 <http://www.americanrhetoric.com/speeches/ronaldreaganbrandenburggate.htm>.

3. Thomas Parrish. *Berlin in the Balance*. Reading, MA: Addison-Wesley, 1998. 1.

Chapter 9. The Aftermath

1. Mohamed ElBaradei. "A World Within Our Grasp." *IAEA.org*. 2004. 27 Nov. 2009. <http://www.iaea.org/Publications/Magazines/Bulletin/Bull472/htmls/nobel2005/world_in_our_grasp.html>.

Index

Index Continued

ABOUT THE AUTHOR

Kayla Morgan lives and writes in New York City. She studied history as an undergraduate and also holds a Master of Fine Arts in writing. In addition to writing books for young readers, Kayla also speaks at schools and conferences around the country, and she teaches writing to teens and adults.

PHOTO CREDITS

Visions LLC/Photolibrary, cover, title page; Hulton Archive, Stringer/Getty Images, 6; AP Images, 11, 17, 18, 27, 28, 35, 36, 46, 54, 59, 64, 67, 78, 97 (top), 98; Red Line Editorial, Inc., 21; Kurt Strumpf/AP Images, 23, 96; Kreusch/AP Images, 41; Romano Cagnoni/Getty Images, 45; Gillhausen/AP Images, 53; DVN/AP Images, 63; Neil Armstrong, NASA/AP Images, 73, 99 (top); U.S. Air Force/AP Images, 69, 97 (bottom); Henry Burroughs/AP Images, 74; Sipa/AP Images, 83, 99 (bottom); Victor Yurchenko/AP Images, 84; Liu Heung Shing/AP Images, 87; Gero Breloer/AP Images, 90; Ron Edmonds/AP Images, 95